UNBOUND BY
TRAUMA

A Soldier's Journey Through
the Scars of Military Sexual
Trauma (MST)

Dr. Laquannia Marshall

No part of this book may be reproduced, stored in a retrieval system, or transmitted in any form or by electronic, mechanical, photocopying, recording, scanning, or otherwise, without the publisher's prior written permission.

Scriptures marked KJV are taken from the KING JAMES VERSION (KJV): KING JAMES VERSION, public domain. They are used with permission - Bible Gateway.com.

ISBN: 978-1954418400
Printed in the United States of America

UNBOUND BY TRAUMA

ACKNOWLEDGMENTS

First, I thank my Lord and Savior, Jesus Christ, for this opportunity and blessing. This opportunity would not be possible without God. God is the Great I Am, and His greatness within me surpasses the greatness of the one who resides in the world.

I want to convey my profound gratitude to my husband, DeAngelo Marshall, for his unwavering love, support, and encouragement and to my beloved sons, John, and Javin.

I would like to express my gratitude to Pastor Bruce C. Hurst for his guidance and heartfelt prayers.

I would like to express my gratitude to Dr. Fredrick Harris for his spiritual mentorship for the past decade.

I would like to thank my publishing team: Jessica AA Highsmith & the Empower Me Books, Incorporated team for a job well done.

PREFACE

The occurrence of military sexual trauma has had a substantial and adverse impact on military members and their families. Comprehending the factors, signs, and underlying structures of sexual assault inside the military is unthinkable. Military Sexual Trauma (MST) leads to various negative consequences such as suppression, substance abuse, suicidal thoughts, and mental health disorders, including Post-Traumatic Stress Disorder (PTSD), anxiety, insomnia, and depression. The author will delve into the powerful emotions and significant repercussions of the highly transformative traumatic event of MST. The author's life is profoundly affected by the lasting scars of MST, probed by unwavering faith.

INTRODUCTION

There is a definite cultural change in the military, with a noticeable lack of understanding regarding the widespread occurrence of military sexual trauma (MST) and the specific factors inside the military that contribute to individuals being susceptible to such situations (Patel). Further actions are necessary to tackle these issues and provide enough support to those who come forward to report. Unfortunately, military personnel in the Armed Forces, who dedicate their lives to protecting and preserving the United States of America both at home and abroad, are faced with the challenges of maintaining their mental well-being and seeking justice in the face of the issue of military sexual trauma. The matter of sexual misbehavior is an ongoing worry for individuals, regardless of their identity, culture, rank, or gender. The potential for causing pain and grief among service members is significant. According to Patel's research, the 2019 Pentagon report on sexual assault inside the military emphasized the ongoing existence of this problem. In 2018, over 20,500 military members experienced incidents of sexual assault, demonstrating a substantial 38% increase compared to the numbers documented in 2016 (Patel).

In an age where sin is commonplace, taking solace in the sovereignty of God is the way, the truth, and the life. Through the power of God's sovereignty, victory can be achieved, even in the aftermath of military sexual trauma. Now, faith is confidence in what we hope for and assurance about what we do not see (Hebrews 11:1). This faith can heal the wounds of sadness, disappointment, and hardship, enabling one to understand that the Lord is always nearby. The Lord will always guide you; he will satisfy your needs in a sun-scorched land and strengthen your frame. You will be like a well-watered garden, like a spring whose waters never run dry (Isaiah 58:11).

The scars caused by military sexual trauma might appear as enduring marks of PTSD, anxiety, depression, insomnia, and other associated disorders. Still, scars can be defined as the result of God's sovereignty, providing healing, direction, and protection, which instills hope that all will eventually be purposeful. Therefore, one will endure the sin, the crime, and the failure of a broken system. Still, God is working it out for His good. As Commanders continue to face difficulties, effectively pushing for disciplinary action against perpetrators implicated in these occurrences, God is still in control. I effectively overcame the scars and wounds of military sexual trauma, resulting in not only my survival but also positively influencing other individuals through Christ, who strengthened me. Military sexual trauma has a profound influence on the daily lives of warriors. Nonetheless, in such circumstances, it is crucial to remember that the Lord's presence is everlasting. My presence will go with you, and I will give you rest (Exodus 33:14). Hence, a believer never has to despair.

CHAPTER 1

A Soldier's Story

My aim for writing this book is to captivate the reader's attention and guide you through the perspective of a survivor who has witnessed the aftermath of wartime trauma through my encounter. This authentic yet vulnerable narrative will illustrate the Army's seeming lack of concern for troops who bear the physical and emotional scars inflicted by their superiors and individuals of influence despite the resources, programs, and wartime concentration at their disposal. Each victim narrative is distinct and exceptional; however, what is consistent is that the force has, in some way or another, failed to adequately safeguard brave Soldiers who are prepared to make the ultimate sacrifice for their nation. I will take one into a comprehensive journey of the accounts my soul can supply on how faith has guided me through military sexual trauma. I will discuss my experiences, from deployment to redeployment, to permanent changes of station (PCS), talking with therapists, counselors, Sexual Harassment and

Assault Response Program representatives, and Veterans Affairs assistance, as well as being diagnosed with PTSD, anxiety, depression, and sleep disturbances. Readers will discover how I, the author, successfully dealt with the trauma and, through faith and hard work, became a minister and school counselor after retiring from the military.

Through this gut-wrenching story, based on factual occurrences, one will discover effective strategies to overcome challenges, adapt, and successfully transition to a new normal. Life is not always filled with a basket of fragrant flowers, but one can find solace in placing confidence in the Lamb of God. He provides guidance and instruction on embodying the rose through scripture, prayer, words of affirmation, and hymnals. One engulfed religious invocation, spiritual songs, affirming verses, and routine prayers during deployment, PCS, redeployment, spousal support, retirement, and life beyond military service daily. This life-altering event regrettably transformed my existence into a spiritual formation in accordance with God's Kingdom. CHAPTER 1

CHAPTER 2

Deployment

As I reflect on my life-altering encounter with the devil in Afghanistan, my emotions are deeply stirred. My eyes fill with tears, and my heart pangs for those who were unable to withstand the overpowering thoughts that engulf the mind and life after returning from such a horrific encounter. I inevitably contemplate the female and male comrades who were tragically lost due to suicide because of military sexual trauma. This story is tailored for people now enduring and confronting the difficulties of involuntarily reconstructing their lives following the encounter with this substantial adversity. While deployed in Afghanistan, I possessed a keen sense of assurance and was well-prepared to participate in combat operations. Our team had diligently trained in our home base, ensuring we were thoroughly prepared for whatever problems we encountered in Afghanistan. My Commanders had extensive knowledge of counterinsurgency methods, yet they remained oblivious to the fact that one of their highest-ranking officers was both a perpetrator and an antagonist. I never anticipated falling prey to such a traumatic experience. Nevertheless, as the events transpired, the perpetrator meticulously devised a strategy to trap me within a confined area, rendering my pleas for assistance futile. Upon the dissipation of the noises, my physical being became enveloped in a state of complete insensitivity. I experienced a heightened intensity in my respiration as though I were endeavoring to evade a dangerous predator, indicating my engagement in a fierce struggle to safeguard myself.

Nevertheless, the devil triumphed and prevailed in the deeds of military sexual trauma. I am not sure how I successfully left the chamber that night. But I found myself back in my tent, utterly devastated, overwhelmed with terror, and considering the possibility of self-harm. Several workdays passed without anybody bothering to check on my well-being despite my daily reports of being unwell. I eventually mustered the strength to pretend that nothing had occurred. At that time, the military focused on training Soldiers in defensive and offensive methods, overlooking the need to train service members to recognize and understand the enemy forces present among the ranks of the Armed Forces.

Therefore, being retraumatized, ashamed, and embarrassed, I chose not to confide in anybody. I repressed my thoughts and feelings via unwavering faith. I carefully devised a plan for navigating my life while harboring this burdensome secret. Throughout the deployment, I confidently relied on a method that involved words of affirmation, prayer, scripture reading, and hymns that I use today to get through the scars of military sexual trauma. My anguish and suffering seemed to gradually diminish through every song, scripture, prayer, and word of affirmation while surrounded in the presence of the Lord. By entrusting my faith in the Lord, I quickly discovered that straying from my well-organized spiritual routines would lead to disorder in my everyday existence. I longed for Christ like a deer thirsting for water every day and every hour. As the deer pants for streams of water, so my soul pants for you, my God (Psalms 42:1). Life transformed into a somber abyss akin to the depths of a cave. As I spent time in the presence of the Lord, I acquired the ability to express my desire to surrender to Him in all things. I depended entirely on Jesus for my survival through the scriptures, prayer, hymnal, and words of affirmation described below.

Scripture

Now, there was a day when the sons of God came to present themselves before the LORD, and Satan also came among them. The LORD said to Satan, "From where have you come?" Satan answered the LORD, saying, "From going to and fro on the earth, and from walking up and down on it." And the LORD said to Satan, "Have you considered my servant Job, that there is none like him on the earth, a blameless and upright man, who fears God and turns away from evil" (Job 6-8).

Prayer

Dear Lord, God, Heavenly Father,
I know you love me. I know you are sovereign. Please lead and guide me during this time of deep pain and agony. Give me the strength of Job who said that even though He slay me, I will trust Him (Job 13:15). I am aware that you were present with Job. Please help me exhibit Job's patience and resilience. I hate my abuser. I need thee. Amen!

Hymn

A Mighty Fortress Is Our God

"And though this world, with devils filled, should threaten to undo us,
We will not fear, for God has willed his truth to triumph through us.
The prince of darkness grim, we tremble not for him;
His rage we can endure, for lo! His doom is sure;
One little word shall fell him."
(Martin Luther, 1529, based on Psalm 46); Translated by (Hedge)

Words of Affirmation

When I am weak, He is Strong! Be a conqueror!

CHAPTER 3

Redeployment

After coming back from deployment, I expected to feel emancipated. Nevertheless, I realized that my body had become reliant on self-determination since the sense of emancipation never materialized. I underwent reintegration every day, eagerly anticipating the swift passage of time, like a cheetah chasing its prey, so that I might return home to tranquility. I did not have to deal with a combat buddy using the same shower, sleeping only steps away from the next Soldier, smelling the unpleasant odor of unclean laundry, or caught in a dust storm that made me anxious since it was difficult to see anyone or anything around. I desired to be in the familiar and safe environment of my own home. Reintegration asserts that the service member undergoes three phases over the reunion period: return, readjustment, and reintegration. During the post-deployment reintegration process, the return phase involves the expectation and the actual physical reunion of those separated. This stage may return quite stressful since there have been changes in both the service member and their family throughout the separation. There is a sense of uncertainty about what these changes could be and how they will be addressed. I preferred not to rehash the horrible situations I endured by choosing to retain my thoughts and emotions privately. The physicians failed to question my experience with military sexual trauma, even during the reintegration process. While acknowledged, deployments to combat or non-combat activities may be highly stressful, the difficulties faced by service members and their families upon returning home sometimes receive less focus (post-deployment reintegration). I assumed that throughout the reintegration process, the medical personnel would ask about war wounds, mental health, and any other injuries that rendered someone unable to function, but the inquiry never came. The well-being of Soldiers themselves poses an additional problem upon their return home. Families expressed worry and uncertainty over symptoms such as social withdrawal, changes in mood, feeling disconnected, and difficulties with sleep (post-deployment reintegration). A single reintegration process included immunizations, risk evaluations, visual and auditory tests, a thorough examination for PTSD, financial considerations, and a checklist.

At the time, reintegration was only a perfunctory obligation to expedite the return of Soldiers to training. The readjustment phase is when military members and their families adapt their behavior to reintegrate into a shared lifestyle (post-deployment reintegration). As stated, every family member will have changed during the separation. The readjustment stage entails acknowledging these changes and giving oneself time to develop a sense of balance (post-deployment reintegration). The approach I received during reintegration was never adequately executed to assist in accurately assessing my mental health. What an utterly faulty system! As a result, I wholeheartedly adopted suppression as the optimal strategy to advance my profession.

Suppression is a legitimate phenomenon; some individuals experience the suppression of distressing occurrences. However, a little spark has the potential to completely alter the situation and trigger individuals to openly drawback in various environments due to the disturbing experience. If triggered, incautiously one sociable life is negatively impacted, a loss of ability to skillfully manage how to be home alone without fear and overcome the challenge of being in a male-dominated profession. I often discovered myself abruptly on high alert, with a combination of apprehension, anxiety, and remorse. Anxiety, guilt, and trust are all intricately linked.

Consequently, I encountered challenges in trusting others and started distancing myself from social interactions. I found trust in my strategy. It was beneficial throughout the deployment, so I returned to the reliable method. Therefore, whenever I felt a rush of adrenaline in my chest and a faster heartbeat, I would confidently turn to prayer, read scripture, sing praise songs, and practice positive self-affirmation, as listed below.

Scripture

For God hath not given us the spirit of fear; but of power, love, and a sound mind (II Timothy 1:7).

Prayer

Dear God and Heavenly Father,
You have not given me a spirit characterized by fear but rather by a healthy and sound mind. I shall not dread any evil because your rod and staff protect me. You are my source and light. I am a divine creation, and everything you have crafted is good. Protect my heart and mind with your word, my Lord. Amen!

Hymn

God, Our Help in Ages Past
"Under the shadow of your throne
Your saints have dwelt secure;
Sufficient is your arm alone,
And our defense is sure."
(Isaac Watts, 1719, based on Psalm 90:1–5)

Words of Affirmation

Be what God destined one to be. Follow Him!

CHAPTER 4

Permanent Change of Station (PCS)

After spending years in my current unit, I was scheduled to PCS, which pleased me. According to "Stand To," a Permanent Change of Stations (PCS) occurs when a Soldier or civilian is instructed to move from one duty station to another for 20 weeks or more. The relocation process begins with orders, which establish a Soldier's entitlements according to their rank, dependent status, basic tour information, and restrictions on what may be brought to the following duty site ("Stand To"). PCSing involves moving on from the past and embracing the new.

I had anticipated that a shift in surroundings, individuals, and locations would lead to a personal metamorphosis. Regrettably, this transition never came to fruition. I realized that I was becoming increasingly annoyed and upset with myself. As I pondered my ideas throughout the attack, my time at my recent assignment was turmoil. I have consistently harbored animosity against everyone, even myself. One day, I received training on Sexual Assault and Sexual Harassment Prevention (SHARP) in my unit.

During the course, I started to experience a sense of liberation while listening to the presenter's words. I have never had such a profound sense of independence and release in any prior military SHARP training, except for one problem. The manifestation of my trauma became increasingly evident, causing me great embarrassment. As the presenter proceeded, I had a powerful sensation of warmth spreading through my entire being like a roaring inferno. Simultaneously, my eyes started to swell, reminiscent of a wasp sting. The presenter firmly said that people with criminal histories and conduct inside our units and organizations need to be responsible for their acts. We have extensive knowledge of SHARP situations, and immediate action taken.

The SHARP Program promotes reporting, conducts complete investigations of any claims of sexual assault and complaints of sexual harassment, and ensures perpetrators are held responsible in an appropriate manner. The lecturer emphasized the need to speak out if one sees something since it is unacceptable. I confidently left the training and headed toward the barracks, where I could not help but cry tears like a child. I had a keen sense of justice and felt confident in seeking help. I expressed my thoughts to both the presenter and mental health counselor. Nevertheless, when I mustered the self-assurance to converse with the presenter days later, I realized, I was looked upon in high regard inside my unit and held a position of authority. I refrained from discussing my trauma since doing so would reveal my lack of confidence and inability to defend myself at the time of the MST. I aimed to prevent any perception of weakness as I currently managed Troopers that depended on me. When I visited the counselor, I confidently shared my experience as a vulnerable soldier. The counselor's body language, lack of compassion, and unprepared manner for circumstances like military sexual trauma resulted in traumatization. I continued the spiritual pursuits that I had initially undertaken in Afghanistan. I found great solace in the initial hope and relief, but unfortunately, it turned into disappointment and demoralization. Both individuals lacked the essential abilities and core understanding required to manage a SHARP case effectively and provide accurate reports. I once again found solace in Jesus Christ with the following practices below:

Scripture

Would not God discover this? For he knows the secrets of the heart Psalm (44:21).

Prayer

Dear God, Heavenly Father,

You knew me in my mother's wound. You made me, and what you made is good. Please help me keep your words in my heart as a reminder that I am good. Please help me to realize that I am not damaged goods. I am your sound, and I will make it through this painful secret that is eating away at my mental health. Amen!

Hymn

Abide with Me

"I fear no foe with thee at hand to bless,
I'll have no weight and tears, no bitterness.
Where is death's sting? Where, grave, thy victory?
I triumph still if thou abide with me."
(Henry Francis Lyte, 1847)

Words of Affirmation

I am beautiful and wonderfully made by the hands of our Creator! I am good.

CHAPTER 5

Permanent Change of Station (PCS)

After three years at my duty station, I learned on a hot summer day in Texas that I would return to the post near the unit I had deployed with to Afghanistan. I hesitated between shedding tears or making a fast getaway like a thief in the night. I did not want to confront the fear of seeing the same buildings and training places where the perpetrator and I trained together. I was aware of the significant consequences that awaited me when I came face-to-face with either the culprit or the leaders of that unit who failed to prioritize my well-being. Within the esteemed Division of Paratroopers, PCS was seldom due to the unique training required by the Airborne community, which cannot be allocated owing to the mission. The President of the United States relies on this Division to be deployed within 18 hours' notice. The Airborne community comprises Soldiers who have received training in the art of parachuting from aircraft.

As a result, addressing Soldier difficulties was

burdensome. It was constantly an environment of high-velocity training to make ready for combat. Paratroopers appeared like robotic machines dedicated to warfare, devoid of human qualities. The display of human emotions such as worry, sympathy, and empathy was absent. The Army's slogan, "Be All You Can Be," was a facade. It was everything the Army had to be, whether in the dungeon or on beach sand. The Army and its purpose are prioritized primarily. The Army's vision was excellent since it challenged the notion that Soldiers and their families are prioritized in the military, revealing a contrasting reality through actions.

I successfully progressed through the ranks with high effectiveness and efficiency with internal darkness. I excelled as a Soldier and Officer, demonstrating great qualities and balancing my family and career. The Army would undoubtedly recognize my achievements at every level. As I contemplated my problems and persevered in life following MST, I could not help but question the nature of excellence. I gained tremendous respect in my organizations, and my children flourished academically and personally despite enduring deployments. I appreciated my spouse, who was highly supportive, God fearing, passionately devout, loving, sensitive, and ambitious. Although we shared a deep affection, he remained oblivious to the significant emotional anguish and wounds that afflicted me daily. I desperately protected my family from the evil snares of my MST at all costs. I had mastered the art of effectively managing a family, soldiering, and rejecting and suppressing my emotions.

According to Veterans Affairs, those who have experienced MST may encounter challenges with attention, concentration, and memory. Service members may struggle to maintain focus and often find their thoughts drifting. Once again, my profound and close bond with God guided me through this period. I utilized the potency of meditation, prayer, music, and positive affirmations to navigate through difficult periods successfully.

Scripture

He lifted me out of the slimy pit, out of the mud and mire; he set my feet on a rock and gave me a firm place to stand (Psalm 40:2).

Prayer

Dear God, Heavenly Father,

You are the potter, and I am the clay. Please continue to keep me as I journey the Army. My days are getting more complex, with some better than others, but please get me to the finish line with good life, health, and strength. And I will forever give your name praise, honor, and glory. Amen.

Hymn

I Will Wait for You (Psalm 130)

"Out of the depths, I cry to You,
In the darkest places, I will call;
Incline Your ear to me anew,
And hear my cry for mercy, Lord."
(Stuart Townend, Keith Getty, Jordan Kauflin, and Matt Merker, 2018)

Words of Affirmation

I am a survivor. I am enough. I am no longer a slave to fear.

CHAPTER 6

Spousal Support

According to Veterans Affairs, military sexual trauma can lead to trust issues, challenges in participating in social activities, and potential concerns with intimacy. Experiencing emotional problems such as guilt, shame, and resentment over the trauma is also a regular occurrence (Veteran Affairs). However, my spouse constantly respected my boundaries and never exerted any pressure on me for physical intimacy. I had relinquished the sensation of closeness and abhorred it. He consistently recognized my need for solitude and honored my boundaries. I sought refuge in my prayer chamber and discovered tranquility amidst the clamor. He consistently offered solace rather than reproaching me when I awoke in tears. I wept due to the torment of never attaining the justice that is rightfully mine.

My spouse highly appreciated my request for him to join me on outings, even while fatigued following a lengthy day at work. He adores me. Husbands, in the same way, be considerate you live with your wives and treat them with respect as the weaker partner and as heirs with you of the gracious gift of life, so that nothing will hinder your prayers

(I Peter 3:7). God meets all needs according to His riches and glory in Christ Jesus (Philippians 4:19). God is omnipresent. Self-harm often penetrated my thoughts, but I am thankful that God safeguarded me. He is unquestionably a source of comfort and peace. He is a wonderful counselor. I triumphed with my steadfast assurance in Jesus. I stretched my hands to thee using the techniques below.

Scripture

> But you, LORD, are a shield around me, my glory, the One who lifts my head high (Psalm 3:3-6).

Prayer

> Dear God, Heavenly Father,
> Thank you for being the lifter of my head. This journey called life is not easy, but I can lean and depend on your outstretched hand that is not waxed short to delivered me from hurt, harm, and danger. I love you. I will forever honor and praise you. Amen

Hymn

Christ Is Mine Forevermore

> "Mine are tears in times of sorrow
> Darkness not yet understood
> Through the valley, I must travel
> Where I see no earthly good
> But mine is the peace that flows from heaven
> And the strength in times of need

I know my pain will not be wasted
Christ completes his work in me."
(Jonny Robinson and Rich Thompson, 2016)

Words of Affirmation

God is the lifter of my head. He is the joy of my strength and need. You got this!

CHAPTER 7

Sexual Harassment and Assault Response Program (SHARP)

Upon arrival at my unit following my PCS, I had the privilege of being acquainted with a civilian SHARP representative. During my years of military duty, I had the opportunity to monitor the Army's SHARP program and observe all representative's knowledge, conduct, and passion for Soldiers. I must say, the civilian SHARP representative was truly unparalleled in my experience. She emitted an aura of brilliance. The Army SHARP program provides Commanders with the essential tools to effectively address and combat sexual assault, sexual harassment, and any subsequent retaliation within the Army (Army Sexual Harassment/Assault Response and Prevention (SHARP) Program).

CHAPTER 8

Finding Relief

I confidently engaged in a conversation with the civilian SHARP representative, seeking genuine and compassionate attributes. Initially, I hesitated to seek assistance from professionals, as I had previously encountered a harsh situation in Texas where the staff showed a lack of adequate training, professionalism, and empathy for sufferers of MST. The interaction just further intensified the stress and psychological anguish I was already enduring. However, after six months of meticulous observations, I was completely ready to disclose my narrative to pursue the justice that had evaded me. I was pleased the morning I decided to meet with the civilian SHARP representative. I arose and participated in physical fitness training. I accomplished a rigorous six-mile run and actively participated in weight training.

After completing my morning exercise routine, I assertively took my place in the representative office at mid-morning. The meeting was really empowering. I keenly observed the representative's contrition, enabling me to recognize genuine care, which was liberating considering my circumstances. I shared my experience and wept because, at last, I was able to confide in someone without the fear of being rejected, disbelieved or the story being shared at my expense. The civilian SHARP representative accurately informed me of the Army's reporting processes for both restricted and unrestricted reporting in a compassionate manner. Given my position, I elected restricted reporting since I was not fully prepared to confront uncertainty. However, it appears that once my report was acknowledged, my mental health plummeted to its lowest point again. I experienced feelings of impurity, insignificance, emotional detachment, frigidity, and confusion. I lacked a sense of identity. I was not pleased with this new version of myself. I chose to discontinue my conversation with the civilian SHARP representative temporarily. However, the individual continued to help me with unwavering patience and understanding.

The individual was a divine blessing and a heavenly presence. For years, leaders neglected to invest time in understanding Soldiers problems despite spending endless hours together and sharing unique life experiences. The human aspect was utterly absent. Nevertheless, I expressed gratitude to God for the existence of civilians working in the Armed Forces. It proved a need for unbiased presence in the Armed Forces. I had no interest in ever sharing or telling my encounter with a green suiter again. I went into praise and worship.

Scripture

Indeed, he will save you from the fowler's snare and the deadly pestilence (Psalm 91:3).

Prayer

Dear God, Heavenly Father,
You love me like you love Abraham. You said faith pleases you, and I thank you, Lord, for your patience with me to trust, believe, and have faith in your outstretched arm. You are good. You are better than good. I praise and worship you forever. Amen.

Hymn

There Is a Hope

"There is a hope that lifts my weary head,
A consolation strong against despair,
That when the world has plunged me into its most bottomless pit,
I find the Savior there!
Through present sufferings, future fear,
He whispers 'courage' in my ear.
For I am safe in everlasting arms,
And they will lead me home."
(Stuart Townend and Mark Edwards, 2007)

Words of Affirmation

God is the author and the finisher of my faith. No adversary can destroy what God meant for good. You are a fighter. Victory is yours!

CHAPTER 9

Meeting the Chaplain

I was introduced to the unit Chaplain as a resource, but my spiritual discernment led me to avoid the Chaplain. After conversing with the Chaplain at my unit, I quickly discerned that despite his role as one of the Commander's top counsels, he could not maintain the confidentiality of my trims. Chaplains should only alert Commanders of issues if they are urgent (Army). Nonetheless, even the Chaplain's role is a dubious resource for victims seeking secrecy in the military.

According to the Army, chaplains serve as spiritual advisers, offering support, encouragement, and emotional direction to Soldiers and their families. The chaplain's responsibilities included addressing the spiritual requirements of every Soldier, both domestically and while on deployment, as well as acknowledging the daily physical, emotional, and spiritual obstacles that Soldiers encounter. Utilize innovative methods in counseling, spiritual guidance, religious initiatives, and support offerings (Army).

CHAPTER 10

Meeting the Therapist

The civilian SHARP representative connected me with a skilled therapist who showed a commendable degree of professionalism. The therapist was deeply fond of the Lord and often spoke about His goodness. I immediately noticed a boost in my spirits and enthusiastically looked forward to meeting with the therapist daily. The therapeutic strategies employed helped me temporarily alleviate concern, sadness, uneasiness, and the difficulties associated with being in a predominantly male atmosphere during the concise 45-minute session. Every session empowered me to regain my sense of self, as well as my self-esteem and dignity. I had cognitive behavior therapy, which effectively helped me reframe my thinking from negative to positive. Cognitive behavioral therapy (CBT) is a powerful psychotherapy treatment that enables patients to identify and alter detrimental thought patterns that affect their behavior and emotions (Cherry).

CHAPTER 11

Transferring Units

Upon fulfilling my duties in the current unit, I was ordered to transfer to a different unit due to my recent promotion to a more senior role. Specifically, I was reassigned to the Division of Paratroopers. Fear coursed through my body like a spark igniting in a densely forested region under strong gusts of wind. I perceived the culture to be uniformly homogeneous, and I harbored concerns that my integration endeavors would be undermined, leading to a regression into feeling alienated and disoriented. I expressed my reservations, but I assertively engaged in a discussion about the subject with my therapist and the SHARP representative.

The SHARP representative assured continuous services from the SHARP representative and the therapist with the highest professionalism and integrity. In such cases, it is normal for Soldiers to be allocated new healthcare professionals upon transferring units. Replacing the therapists and SHARP representatives assigned to the unit or organization is customary when shifting units. However, I effectively maintained the integrity of the individuals I interacted with, ensuring a smooth transition in one's emotional well-being and mental health status.

I successfully reported to my new job and familiarized myself with the new boss. Leadership is skillfully guiding and motivating others to accomplish a job. In the Army, the Commander and their leadership style directly impact a unit's success or failure (Falce). The initial impression of the working atmosphere was positive, with individuals with great character and a strong work ethic.

The toxicity became apparent with the advent of a new boss. He had traits of narcissism. When narcissism traits become extremely evident, Leaders produce a toxic environment (Lafalce). The new boss had a significant impact on my emotional well-being. While working, I experienced a profound feeling of confinement, as being confined in the same space as my perpetrator. Whenever my boss would call, I would promptly have a migraine headache. While engaging in physical fitness exercises, I felt nausea and fatigue in his presence.

During that period, the leader's detrimental conduct affected the department in my unit. The officers in my sector courageously endured the toxic actions of our Boss. Regrettably, my history of trauma had an impact on my capacity to manage the poison. Lafalce's perspective on toxic leadership asserts that Commanders place utmost importance on achieving victory, even to the point of considering Soldiers as dispensable. There are indeed effective strategies available to manage a toxic boss, but I have never had the resolve to confront a narcissist or the capacity to impede their professional progress. I have meticulously recorded instances involving this superior which persuaded me to formally denounce his actions to the Commanding General. However, I was reminded by the divine that punishment falls under His authority.

The rise of this new leader sparked a potent combination of anger and resolve inside me as I realized that I could no longer endure the disrespectful and undignified behavior of Leaders who prioritize their careers and self-interests over Soldiers. I took the initiative to reach out to my SHARP representative to elevate my previously restricted report to an unrestricted one. I requested aid in ensuring justice was obtained for the injustices that were perpetrated on me as a young vulnerable Soldier. As a Warrant Officer, I held a strong conviction in pursuing justice for myself and all other military service members who merit equitable treatment, neutrality, and equal status.

Regrettably, Leaders often demonstrate bigotry and intolerance toward both women and men. Only a select few military members have the fortitude to confront such disrespectful behavior as they strive to prevent misery and persevere through ongoing and arduous suffering. This sort of abusive conduct often follows a consistent pattern.

Upon consulting with the lawyer, I have ascertained that the statute of limitations expired for reporting the MST event that happened years ago. Upon receiving the devastating news, I was momentarily left without words. I found myself confined within a cage with no viable methods of liberation. Considering my mental health condition, my therapist decided to recommend me to the Army's treatment clinic specifically designed for Soldiers diagnosed with PTSD and who encountered MST.

CHAPTER 12

Mental Health Challenges

Based on the medical record data from Veteran Affairs, depression and other mood disorders are frequently associated with MST among VA healthcare customers, in addition to PTSD. According to the data provided by the VA, it is evident that both military and civilian sexual assault survivors have a higher occurrence of PTSD throughout their lives, with men at 65 percent and females at 49.5 percent. Due to the challenging presence of the new toxic boss in my unit, my life took a tumultuous turn, with my aspirations growing stronger, causing me to struggle with sleeplessness as I pondered whether I would ever find peaceful repose. The nightmares gathered considerable momentum and were remarkably vivid. I began to perceive a powerful sensation of someone endeavoring to apprehend me. My nervousness heightened and hampered me from establishing trust in people and stepping out freely.

Depression infiltrated and convinced me that life lacked significance and had no inherent worth. Every day brought out a formidable adventure I faced head-on as

I confronted every individual. There was a deficiency in the domain of social relationships. It was important to consistently be watchful and practice prudence to guarantee the safety of one's children, as there may be those who warrant suspicion. There was a persistent feeling of uneasiness and uncertainty about what the following day could bring. The days were consistent with a state defined by sorrow and suffering. MST results in an enduring condition of emotional distress when individuals are trapped in a state of intense pain, anguish, and the constant relieving and retriggering of past traumatic experiences. Managing internal battles may be a formidable task, especially when faced with toxic leaders at the unit level.

CHAPTER 13

Coping

I was provided with strategies to manage the challenges of internal and negative work environments effectively. The Veterans Affairs Handbook states strategies include getting professional help, making lifestyle changes, practicing mindfulness, fostering optimism, connecting with peers, considering emotional support animals, and investigating available options. Seeking the support of a counselor or therapist who specializes in sexual trauma, based on the information supplied by the VA, can be a highly beneficial beginning step toward healing.

Participating in lifestyle modifications, such as connecting with other individuals who have encountered military sexual trauma, adhering to a consistent exercise regimen, embracing a nutritious diet, and engaging in volunteer work, can also yield positive outcomes. Incorporating mindfulness, which is being conscious and concentrated on the current moment and fostering optimism by actively searching for good elements in one's life that offer joy, serenity, or contentment, is a supplementary technique that can enhance overall well-being. Engaging with peer groups of persons who have experienced MST might provide a reassuring environment for addressing this shared experience. Furthermore, some individuals discover comfort in emotional support animals, which can effectively reduce stress in circumstances that might otherwise be overpowering. It is advantageous to additionally consider alternate choices and maintain an open mindset toward discovering answers. I have not yet found solace in these coping strategies.

I have gained a deep understanding of mindfulness and the power to transform my mindset by embracing the spiritual teachings of Jesus Christ. Therefore, I urge you, brothers, and sisters, in view of God's mercy, to offer your bodies as a living sacrifice, holy and pleasing to God— this is your true and proper worship (Romans 12:1). Therefore, one should embrace the decision to not conform to the ways of this world but rather open one's mind to a spiritual formation. Spiritual formation provides a perpetual source of inspiration and a consistent nurturing relationship with the Word of God. Whoever believes in me, as Scripture has said, rivers of living water will flow from within them (John 7:38). I long to acquire that life-giving water as the Samaritan woman did when she met Jesus at the well. The woman said to him, "Sir, give me this water so that I won't get thirsty and have to keep coming here to draw water (John 4:15)". John 4:15 guarantees that whatever obstacles I encounter, my life will be dynamic and prepared to flourish.

CHAPTER 14

The Army's Patriot Program

Due to the detrimental environment, I experienced at my unit I was reassigned to collaborate closely with the esteemed counselors and physicians of the Army's Patriot Program. The program has equipped me with the necessary resources to finally find solace after years of enduring mental health pain. Thanks to this program, I have acquired an elevated level of skill and proficiency in self-care methodologies, such as hot yoga treatment, cognitive behavioral therapy, art therapy, and music therapy. I have successfully developed the ability to identify my triggers. I possess the necessary proficiency to address any trigger I encounter effectively.

This program enabled me to confidently share my experiences with a community of others who have encountered comparable obstacles, such as memory impairment, worry, sadness, PTSD, sleep disturbances, and distressing dreams. One adeptly copes with the obstacles of circumventing grocery stores and handling relationships for a substantial duration. The program was entirely satisfactory. During the program, I witnessed a tremendous revelation in which God disclosed that my life transcends my mere existence. I have unequivocally determined that I have personally experienced and witnessed disconcerting occurrences.

I assisted my fellow peers in the Army's Patriot Program by supporting them in identifying their triggers and navigating through periods of poor emotional deterioration. I have effectively instructed, advised, and guided Soldiers under my supervision for over 20 years. I have come to comprehend that every single event I have had during my professional journey has played a pivotal role in God's grand design to fashion and refine me into a resounding voice, an influential figure, a trusted advisor, and a servant of His divine realm. "For I know the plans I have for you," declares the Lord, "plans to prosper you and not to harm you, plans to give you hope and a future" (Jeremiah 29:11).

To assist God's children successfully and efficiently with power, strength, and anointed hands, one must possess a narrative, a personal tale in which reliance on Jesus was necessary to overcome the problems of the spirit, mind, and body. Thomas asserts with conviction that a genuine comprehension of the unfathomable intricacies of another individual's essence can only be attained through personal tribulations. I have successfully endured. Undoubtedly, it is within God's divine design for me to now achieve the highly regarded commission in Him. God is fully deserving of all the praise, honor, and glory.

Consequently, I decided to retire from the United States Army, commence my pursuit of a Master of Arts in Pastoral Counseling degree, and transfer into the field of counseling. The LORD makes firm the steps of the one who delights in him (Psalm 37:23). I discovered that the Lord was preparing me for my next assignment in the Army of the Lord as I completed the Army's Patriot Program. Despite enduring adversity in the military, my suffering was never in futility. The light beneath my path was God. No one journeys through life for their benefit. Jesus did not come to earth to do the same; His purpose was to save humanity.

CHAPTER 15

Retirement from the Army

I was ill-equipped to transition out of the Army, because of the harrowing ordeal I endured and the untimely demise of my mother. Upon deciding to retire, I found myself consumed by an overwhelming sense of anguish and loss. I deemed it imperative to give precedence to the welfare of myself, my family, and the Army by opting for retirement. Upon contemplation of the past, I cannot help but speculate whether the incidence of the MST might have averted had I adhered to my initial intention of remaining for 30 years. I shall never ascertain, as a malefactor deprived me of that prerogative. I have absolutely no regrets regarding my service in the military since it has significantly enhanced the welfare of my family and our entire standard of living through materialistic advantages and health benefits.

Soldiers and Commanders who possess commendable character are akin to a close-knit family. I vividly remember how the Christmas events and social gatherings immensely contributed to easing the feeling of being away from home. Together, we shared a common fate as comrades in the military. Therefore, I will never experience any remorse when devoting myself to a nation that I deeply cherish. Only individuals with malicious motives and unlucky circumstances befall people with virtuous aspirations. I shall forever remain steadfast in my unwavering allegiance to the Almighty, fully assured of His supreme authority, even in moments of perplexity when the rationale behind events eludes me. Upon my departure from the service, I steadfastly retained a sanguine outlook. I have faith in God to get a renewed sense of importance and a purposeful new beginning.

My retirement period happened to align with the commencement of the COVID-19 epidemic. During the national emergency, all North Carolina residents were mandated to remain in their homes. During that period, I transformed my home into a place of prayer and dedicated myself to personal growth. I exercised daily. I practiced meditation daily. I dedicated time to journaling and spent a significant amount of time in reflection with the Lord.

After time, the military was issued instructions to resume duty, at which point I discerned that opting for retirement was the most prudent decision. Resuming my activities after the outbreak disturbed my mental health. Reverting to such a detrimental setting seemed incongruous with the trajectory of embracing recovery. As a result, I successfully fulfilled the Transition Assistance Program (TAP) requirements and obtained an honorable discharge from the military within 18 months. The Army TAP is the Army's program that guarantees Soldiers get the essential counseling, job, and education courses and seminars to fulfill the Career Readiness Standards (CRS) mandated by law and policy ("Army Transition Assistance Program TAP").

TAP has undergone a comprehensive re-engineering process to optimize the training and connection of Soldiers, enhancing their prospects for attaining personal and professional success outside of the military. Upon concluding active duty, I felt a sense of gratitude having successfully completed the race. The military proved to be a formidable endeavor. I departed with commendable honor. Completing the assignment is crucial to fully enjoy the prizes and blessings that Christ has prepared for us (Wilson). The benefits and blessings have been continuously pouring onto me and my family. Wilson confidently states that as Christians, we must persist and complete our faith journey with a purposeful mindset, demonstrating unwavering tenacity and discipline.

Despite not having had my day in court, I am confident I can persevere in facing the opposition. I had completed the assignment and proclaimed to the world the greatness of the Lord and all the blessings he bestowed upon me. I have fought the good fight, I have finished the race, I have kept the faith (II Timothy 4:7). I had successfully overcome the spiritual challenges surrounding me during my military tenure. For our struggle is not against flesh and blood, but against the rulers, against the authorities, against the powers of this dark world, and against the spiritual forces of evil in the heavenly realms (Ephesians 6:12). I would like to mention the scripture, prayer words and affirmation, and hymnal that I relied on to stay focused throughout that period of my life.

Scripture

Therefore, take up the whole armor of God so that you can resist in the evil day, and having done everything, stand firm (Ephesians 6:13).

Prayer

Dear God and Heavenly Father,
I have found a favor in your sight that you help me finish this race. My soul cries hallelujah for your grace and mercy and sovereignty over me! Thank you for blessing me to see this momentous time in my life. I will forever give your name praise and honor. Amen!

Hymnal

Praise to the Lord, the Almighty

"Praise to the Lord, who o'er all things so wondrously reigneth,
Shelters thee under his wings, yea, so gently sustaineth!
Hast thou not seen how thy desires ever have been
Granted in what he ordaineth?"
(Joachim Neander, 1680); Translated by
(Catherine Winkworth, 1863)

Words of Affirmation

God made the best. I am the best. I am worthy. I can do all things through Christ who strengthens me.

CHAPTER 16

Earning A Master of Arts in Pastoral Counseling

Sharma states that pastoral counseling combines psychological and religious counseling. It integrates clinical psychology techniques with spiritual resources to promote healing and personal development (Sharma). A pastoral counselor is a highly skilled mental health practitioner with extensive religious, theological, and spiritual expertise (Sharma). I was pleased with this description of the pastoral counselor since my earlier experiences had prepared me for what to anticipate, thanks to God. Pastoral counselors assist individuals in distress by utilizing prayer, teaching from scripture, and encouraging community involvement, guiding individuals toward healing and personal growth (Sherma).

Enrolling in the Master of Arts in Pastoral Counseling at Liberty University was a beneficial decision. Liberty's Pastoral Counseling Program provided me with a comprehensive understanding of the psychological and biological impacts of my diagnosis. Thomas asserts that counseling is a means to assist people in achieving the life God has intended. The thief comes only to steal and kill and destroy; I have come that they may have life and have it more abundantly (John 10:10).

I received comprehensive education on all mental health illnesses mentioned in the DSM-5, as well as practical treatment approaches for those experiencing distress. I have comprehensively understood the significance and aspects contributing to one's mental well-being deterioration. I also recognized the necessity for pastoral counseling in the community and the church. Frequently, individuals inside the church seek assistance from external sources for mental health emergencies involving members, friends, and acquaintances. If clergy includes counseling services, support may be found within the church. Surveys of Americans consistently show that religious individuals approach their clergy as a first step when seeking help rather than immediately turning to professionals (Thomas et al.).

I have successfully managed mental anguish solely without needing professional guidance until eventually acquiring the appropriate support. Due to the societal prejudice around mental health, persons may experience the perception that others consider them to be of lesser worth compared to the inherent value they possess as a child of God. The undeniable benefit of counseling lies in its ability to assist individuals in developing a Christ-like character (Thomas et al.). Through my story, His influence persisted, empowering me with assurance as I entered my internship. Upon completing my internship, I discovered my keen sense of calling to serve as a Minister of the Gospel.

Upon completion of my Master of Arts in Pastoral Counseling, I was fortunate to have the opportunity to advise individuals of all ages within the church and outside the church with my pastors' and supervisors' guidance and support. I persevered in my dedication to completing God's purpose for my life, ensuring that I maintained unwavering concentration and commitment throughout the process. I possess the necessary skills to provide spiritual guidance to people across all age groups. I possess a profound comprehension of trauma, grief, and distress.

The Army served as my battleground for successfully overcoming the multitude of offenses on a global scale. The divine fully equipped me to conduct my mission in this earthly realm, notwithstanding the tumultuous nature of my past experiences. The Almighty is perpetually just, with an unwavering focus on His chosen. God has chosen me. He turned my trauma into triumphs.

He turned my assault into acquiescence. He turned my sadness into sanctification. He gives life.

CHAPTER 17

From Pain to Influence

Upon acquiring my graduate degree, I had the privilege of securing a position as a counselor. Christian counselors and pastors have the duty to recognize the inaccuracies in our lives, continuously pursuing God's love, power, and truth and acting as channels of His truth and grace to others who need our help (Hawkins et al.). It is imperative to answer the summons for the chosen individuals promptly. We will confront mortality, wrath, challenges and hardships, letdowns, perplexity, and upheaval.

We might not consistently grasp the obstacles that emerge during life's journey but there is resolution and purpose. God will reveal His divine plan if we have unwavering conviction in our beliefs and faith. Without succumbing to exhaustion, one must remain resolute in doing well, regardless of any obstacle. The governance of all is under the purview of divine providence. He is a ruler who utilizes suffering to aid in executing His

Kingdom's mission. His Kingdom mission took me from pain to powerful, doubtful to decorous, and impotence to influential. He produces winners!

CHAPTER 18

Exhibiting Faith

According to Webster, faith is characterized by unwavering trust and confidence in a reliable divine entity, adherence to established religious principles, and a profound conviction in something that lacks empirical evidence. The Bible instructs us that faith entails an unwavering conviction in our objectives and a robust assurance in the imperceptible. Amidst life's trials, it is natural to question the existence of a greater power and ponder the underlying reasons behind certain events. One may explore the justification for God's support of such circumstances, the seeming lack of justice despite God's professed nature, and the apparent impunity enjoyed by individuals who partake in malevolence.

Other factors may come into play, leading individuals to sometimes question or doubt their religious convictions or faith in higher authority. My comprehension of biblical theology and the engagements with notable individuals in the Bible who have likewise experienced loss, pain, disappointment, and hopelessness have bestowed upon me essential wisdom. One may confidently rely on the Almighty to commit to completing his promises in times of adversity, graciously bestowing rewards upon those who possess firm trust and are utterly incapable of experiencing failure. It is essential to always consider the fundamental ideas and teachings of the Bible, together with the accounts of individuals who have demonstrated unwavering faith. When we send petitions to heaven, God demands nothing more than a modest measure of faith akin to that of a mustard seed. He dutifully attends to our inquiries once we have pardoned those who have transgressed against us. God's character, acts, and actions remain unchanging, and He graciously equips humanity with all the essential tools for spiritual growth to achieve a deep connection with Him.

The LORD offers steadfast direction and support, remaining concrete by one's side and never forsaking them. The Word of God is a promise. Do not be afraid; do not be discouraged (Deuteronomy 31:8). Every person can rely on the unwavering support of divine intervention. God is faithful, who has called you into fellowship with his Son, Jesus Christ our Lord (I Corinthians 1:9).

Faith has garnered favor over prominent biblical figures, notably the woman mentioned in (Luke 8). The Bible noted a woman was there who had been subject to bleeding for twelve years, but no one could heal her (Luke 8:43). She felt utterly weary, disheartened, weak, and lacking any hope in this crucial situation. The woman exhibited an unwavering belief that Jesus had the ability to restore her physical well-being via an act of steadfast faith. With unwavering assurance, she extended her hand and touched the edge of Jesus' robe, encountering a profound restoration. Then he said to her, "Daughter, your faith has healed you. Go in peace (Luke 8:48)."

Throughout my arduous road of grappling with military sexual trauma, I have consistently received unwavering support from the omnipotent power of the Lord's righteous hand. Despite rare moments of discouragement, the voice of the Lord consistently reassured me of His overwhelming grace and new mercies each morning. The presence of the divine remains in spirit and truth. He bestows salvation and everlasting life onto those who keep resolute faith. Undoubtedly, God is dependable and never engages in any injustice. He is the Rock, his works are perfect, and all his ways are just. A faithful God who does no wrong, upright, and just is he (Deuteronomy 32:4).

Embrace the presence of injustices, wrongdoing, and storms of life that accompany military sexual trauma with faith. God will metamorphose you into the optimal manifestation of your being. Persevere in faith despite uncertainty. Persevere in faith when encountering hurt. Persevere in faith through pain. Faith it through!

CONCLUSION

There is no justification for any Soldier to bear the lasting effects of military sexual trauma. Military sexual trauma inflicts a lasting sorrow that cannot be conquered easily. Clinton defines grief as profound emotional distress resulting from a loss. MST resulted in the loss of security and dignity, leading to immediate grief. Grieving is akin to venturing into the depths of a valley, where it entails suffering, effort, and a prolonged journey (Clinton et al.). The phases of grieving consist of denial or shock, anger, bargaining, sadness, and acceptance. However, everything will return to a new normal with the unwavering support of God, who provides healing via His word, love, and fidelity. Grieving is a transformative journey that leads to both healing and personal development ("Emotional Healing and Personal Growth (Spirituality for Beginners 13)").

Healing is achievable, even when justice falls short by some years. One can heal even when one encounters the same setting and perpetrator regularly. You can heal even when you are your only source of comfort. You can heal even when you were near death. You can heal even when others doubt you. You can heal. Greater is He that is in you, than he that is in the world. I have discovered that throughout the Bible, there are instances where individuals like Isaiah served as conduits for God's healing words to the people. For example, Isaiah sent a message from God, urging the people to let go of their past and not fixate on previous events. Behold, I am embarking on a new endeavor! Behold, it arises; do you not discern it, Isaiah (48:18-19)? God bestows upon us the gift of new beginnings in the latter days. No matter the challenges we face, it is of no consequence. Embracing Christ faith is the essence of our life.

The effective functioning of the body, mind, and soul depends on maintaining a state of equilibrium. The balance may seem elusive for military sexual trauma victims due to the irreversible nature of their injuries. However, regaining control over one's thinking is crucial to recovery. A part of individuals may feel lost after experiencing a trauma, but reading the Bible every day assists in reclaiming what was taken. I take immense pleasure in the law of the Lord and contemplate his law consistently, both day and night. Individuals who trust the Lord resemble a tree strategically positioned near flowing streams, producing fruit at the appropriate time, and maintaining healthy leaves that do not wither but thrive, as Ortberg suggests.

The high occurrence of military sexual trauma in the military leads to considerable distress, especially when members engage in acts of sexual misbehavior against one another. According to Clinton and Hawkins (2009), suffering can arise from factors, including personal growth, challenges, and the display of God's greatness, while also playing a vital role in emulating His example. Justice is sometimes elusive for victims in the military, but it is essential to remember that retribution is in the hands of a higher power. God's sovereignty, sufficiency, and faithfulness of His love in judging our enemies, freedom, and forgiveness serve as the fundamental attitude for recuperating and being the person God intended us to be. According to religious beliefs, forgiveness is a reciprocal act where those who provide forgiveness will also receive forgiveness, restoring mental and emotional well-being. When individuals provide forgiveness to others, the divine Father will also reciprocate with forgiveness.

Regarding the biblical passage in Matthew 6:14-15, it is essential to note that if one does not forgive others for their wrongdoings, the Father will not provide forgiveness. Hence, forgiving is crucial for empowerment, healing, and recuperation. We are confident that everything works together for the good of those who love God and are called according to his purpose (Romans 8:28).

I have discovered a profound sense of serenity and affection having a relationship with Jesus Christ, even when I felt as through all hope was lost. Jesus Christ has bestowed upon me dreams, visions, and a promise that affirms the superiority of His presence inside me over the forces of the world. God demonstrated His immense love for the world by giving His only begotten son, enabling me to live a fulfilling life. I am perplexed why my life took such a tumultuous turn, resembling a volcano erupting amid a serene meadow. However, it happened at that moment for a reason. It was not about me; it was about saving others.

God receives glory as I am empowered to proclaim His message and assist people needing scripture, words of affirmation, hymns, or prayers to overcome the grip of mental health illnesses. This testimony has been proven dependable and effective in providing comfort, breakthrough, and support for mental distress and profound disbelief. The reality is that no one can genuinely testify about the experiences of sexual trauma, despair, anxiety, hopelessness, and sleeplessness unless they have personally endured the trials and suffering. My advice is to lead a life that is agreeable to God. Submit life to him daily. He will bravely confront challenges, and just as He did with His faithful servants Job and Elisha, He showered double prosperity. Have faith in navigating life's challenges and witness God's abundant blessings above one's capacity to receive. I can personally attest to His unwavering commitment.

God demonstrated His love by freely offering Jesus on the cross to rescue sinners. He bore our transgressions in his physical form upon the crucifix, granting us liberation from wrongdoing and enabling us to lead a blameless existence. You have been restored by the injuries he endured (1 Peter 2:24). Upon recognizing the supreme authority of the Almighty, an individual's presence on this terrestrial plane becomes imbued with resolute triumph and unassailable conquest. Victory on the cross ensures that no battle is lost in life. Jesus boldly approached them and said, "I have been bestowed with absolute authority in both heaven and earth" (Matthew 28:18-19).

Everyone is obligated to carry their cross daily, just as Jesus carried His through the marketplace to the place of the skull. The weight of enduring the cross serves a meaningful purpose when one lives a life guided by divine leading. Only those who bear their cross and faithfully follow Him have the privilege of being His disciples (Luke 14:27). Embrace the crucifix and ardently desire His divine presence. He will never leave one or forsake one.

As readers can observe, the author experienced a significant setback as a young private in the United States Army, and unfortunately, justice was never served. One has endured a considerable amount of mental, physical, and emotional anguish for an extended period, resulting in the loss of my identity, voice, dignity, and confidence. However, faith restored it all.

"The rehabilitation of profound trauma is represented by restored faith." ~ Dr. Marshall

Daily Checklist for Mental Health:

Following military sexual trauma (MST), individuals often have a tendency for their thoughts to deteriorate into dangerous ideations or suicidal tendencies. However, by reframing one's thinking, one may restore, refresh, and revitalize.

Identify the regions where a downward spiral is occurring and counteract negative ideas by using affirmations and scripture to promote positive thinking and thoughts.

☐ I hate myself .... I deserve self-respect.

☐ I am not worthy .... I am worthy of it all.

☐ I will never be whole again .... I am strong and courageous.

☐ Feeling hopeless .... With God all things are possible!

☐ I do not want to be here .... God loves you.

☐ Doubt .... Faith over doubt.

☐ Feeling fear/anxiety .... Do not fear or be dismayed.

☐ My life will never be the same .... God is the author and finisher of my faith.

☐ Who can I trust, I cannot live like this .... I am trusting God, He will change my life.

Thoughts and observations...

_____

_____

_____

_____

_____

Fruitful thoughts:

You were formed in the flawless image of God. No evil exists that could diminish that perfect image. Behold the metamorphosis of your life as you reclaim control and strength in opposition to the adversary.

Hymnal:

Amazing grace (how sweet the sound)
That saved a wretch like me!
I once was lost, but now am found
Was blind, but now I see

Prayer:

Most High God you are the Creator of my very being. Control my thoughts, my mind, and my soul with your all-powerful hands. I feel weak today, but you are strong. I feel unrest but in you there is rest. I feel lost and hopeless but in you, I am more than a conqueror. I have faith in your wonderful working power. Thank you for hearing and answering my prayers. Amen

"A changed thought can save a life in the midst of a downward spiral moment." ~ Dr. Marshall

REFERENCES

"100% of Military Sexual Assault Survivors Feel 'Trapped,'
    Have Suicidal Ideations." *PBS NewsHour*,
    7 July 2021, www.pbs.org/newshour/show/100-of-
    military-sexual-assault-survivors-feel-trapped-have-
    suicidal-ideations.

"25 Hymns to Sing in Troubled Times." *9Marks*,
    www.9marks.org/article/25-hymns-to-sing-in-
    troubled-times/.

"Army Chaplain." *Goarmy.com*, 10 Sept. 2021,
    www.goarmy.com/careers-and-jobs/specialty-
    careers/chaplain.html.

"Army Sexual Harassment/Assault Response and
    Prevention (SHARP) Program." *Www.army.mil*,
    www.army.mil/article/245382/army_sexual_harass
    mentassault_response_and_prevention_sharp_prog
    ram.

"Army Transition Assistance Program
    (TAP)." *143.84.225.51*,
    myarmybenefits.us.army.mil/Benefit-
    Library/Federal-Benefits/Army-Transition-
    Assistance-Program-(TAP)-.

(n.d.). BibleGateway.com: A searchable online Bible in over
    150 versions and 50 languages.
    https://www.biblegateway.com/ (2023, November
    17).

Clinton, Tim, and Ron Hawkins. *The Quick-Reference Guide
    to Biblical Counseling*. Baker Books, 2009.

Drake, Kimberly. "COVID-19 and Behavior: Effects on
    Mental Health, Communication." *Medical and
    Health Information*,
    www.medicalnewstoday.com/articles/how-has-the-
    pandemic-changed-our-behavior.

"Emotional Healing and Personal Growth (Spirituality for
    Beginners 13)." *Psychology Today*,

www.psychologytoday.com/us/blog/spiritual-wisdom-secular-times/201208/emotional-healing-and-personal-growth-spirituality.

Faith. (n.d.) Merriam-Webster: America's Most Trusted Dictionary. https://www.merriam-webster.com/dictionary/faith

"Handling Toxic Leadership." *Army University Press Home*, www.armyupress.army.mil/Journals/NCO-Journal/Archives/2017/October/Handling-Toxic-Leadership/.

Hawkins, Ron, and Tim Clinton. *The New Christian Counselor: A Fresh Biblical and Transformational Approach.* Harvest House Publishers, 2015.

"How Cognitive Behavior Therapy Works." *Verywell Mind*, 3 Mar. 2009, www.verywellmind.com/what-is-cognitive-behavior-therapy-2795747.

Ortberg, John. *The Me I Want to Be: Becoming God's Best Version of You.* Zondervan, 2010.

Patel, Shaunak. "Military Sexual Assault: Why Are Service Members at Risk and What Can Be Done to Prevent It?" *USC-MSW*, 29 Nov. 2022, msw.usc.edu/mswusc-blog/military-sexual-assault-prevalence-prevention/.

"Postdeployment Reintegration - Strategies to Protect the Health of Deployed U.S. Forces - NCBI Bookshelf." *National Center for Biotechnology Information*, www.ncbi.nlm.nih.gov/books/NBK225083/.

"Rape Victims Prone to Suicide - Suicide.org." *Suicide.org: Suicide Prevention, Suicide Awareness, Suicide Support - Suicide.org! Suicide.org! Suicide.org!*, www.suicide.org/rape-victims-prone-to-suicide.html.

Sharma, Swarnakshi. "Pastoral Counseling: What Is It? Who Can Benefit? How Does It Help?" *Calm Sage - Your Guide to Mental and Emotional Well-being*, 15 July 2021, www.calmsage.com/what-is-pastoral-counseling/.

"STAND-TO!" *Www.army.mil*, 3 May 2019,
www.army.mil/standto/archive/2019/05/03/.

"Stressors: Coping Skills and Strategies." *Cleveland Clinic*,
my.clevelandclinic.org/health/articles/6392-stress-
coping-with-lifes-stressors.

Thomas, John C., and Lisa Sosin. *Therapeutic Expedition:
Equipping the Christian Counselor for the Journey*.
B&H Publishing Group, 2011.

"VA.gov | Veterans Affairs." *PTSD: National Center for
PTSD Home*,
www.ptsd.va.gov/understand/types/sexual_trauma_
military.asp.

"What is MST? Military Sexual Trauma." *DAV*,
25 Sept. 2023, www.dav.org/get-help-
now/veteran-topics-resources/military-sexual-
trauma-mst/.

Wilson, Jamie. "27 Inspiring Bible Verses About Finishing
the Race." *Scripture Savvy*,
scripturesavvy.com/bible-verses-about-finishing-
the-race/.

"'A Poison in the System': The Epidemic of Military Sexual
Assault (Published 2021)." *The New York Times -
Breaking News, US News, World News and Videos*,
11 Oct. 2021,
www.nytimes.com/2021/08/03/magazine/military-
sexual-assault.html.

BOOK REVIEW

BY WILL C. GLASS

"

Unbound by Trauma –The book charts an exploration of resilience, faith, and healing. Anyone interested in those areas will certainly benefit. The universal themes of struggle, faith, and transformation resonate beyond the military, but I see those in the categories below will resonate most
with the material:
Military Personnel and Veterans
Family's members
Advocates and educators
Survivors seeking healing

CW3 (R) Will C. Glass
Raleigh, NC

BOOK REVIEW

BY LOVELLA P. MOGERE

"

Unbound by Trauma – Based on reading the first chapter of this book and my understanding of Sexual Harassment/Assault. This book can be utilized to help Soldiers but more specifically Commanders understand the harm that this action causes not on the individual who experienced it but their Families. Commanders need to read this book before taking command so they can understand their responsibility to ensure that this does not happen within their organization and not just talk about it when we have a requirement/awareness month. Soldiers need to read this while attending Basic Training/Advanced Individual Training, so they truly understand that it's not tolerated and consequences come with their actions.

Officers in ROTC programs, Cadets at West Point, and just every entry-level arrival system we have for individuals entering all Services need to read this book. Sexual Harassment/Assault happens everywhere teenagers at school, colleges, universities, and various work environments. I would like to hope that it won't ever happen to anyone again, however until we know that it has stopped your book can be utilized everywhere so everyone truly understands the individuals and Families suffering and to help stop the pain by educating everyone that this must stop.

CSM (R) Vickie G. Culp
Retire September 2019.
Served 30 years of Active Federal Service

ABOUT THE AUTHOR

Dr. Laquannia Marshall

Is a warrior and survivor, called to empower those impacted by MST!

Dr. Laquannia M. Marshall, a resident of North Carolina, holds the position of associate minister and is a co-owner of Stallion Trucking Services, LLC, DBA Chief's Stable Adventures alongside her spouse, Counselor, and former US Army Chief Warrant Officer Three.

Laquannia, a seminary graduate with a Ph.D. in Biblical Studies, a Master of Arts in Pastoral Counseling from Liberty University, and a Bachelor of Science in Psychology from Excelsior University, regards it as an honor to assist adherents of all faiths and cultures in gaining an intellectual understanding of the truths of Scripture and being encouraged to experience these truths practically through the influence of the Holy Spirit.

Chief's Stable Adventures, a therapeutic horse ministry, was established jointly by Deangelo and Dr. Laquannia Marshall. After dedicating themselves to the nation, the Marshalls aspired to furnish the community with an additional foundation of beneficial resources through their devotion.

Dr. Marshall is married to Retired Chief Warrant Officer Three Deangelo C. Marshall, and they share two beloved sons.

Contact her at: DrMarshallWrites@gmail.com